Guitar Case Chord Book

Project editor: Ed Lozano
Photography by Randall Wallace
Interior design and layout by Mark Bridges

This book Copyright © 2002 by Amsco Publications,
A Division of Music Sales Corporation, New York

All rights reserved. No part of this book may be
reproduced in any form or by any electronic or mechanical means,
including information storage and retrieval systems,
without permission in writing from the publisher.

Order No. AM 974171
US International Standard Book Number: 0.8256.1940.8
UK International Standard Book Number: 0.7119.9444.7

Exclusive Distributors:
Music Sales Corporation
257 Park Avenue South, New York, NY 10010 USA
Music Sales Limited
8/9 Frith Street, London W1D 3JB England
Music Sales Pty. Limited
120 Rothschild Street, Rosebery, Sydney, NSW 2018, Australia

Printed in the United States of America by
Vicks Lithograph and Printing Corporation

Amsco Publications
an imprint of the **Music Sales** *Publishing Group*
NEW YORK/LONDON/PARIS/SYDNEY/COPENHAGEN/MADRID

table of contents

The frames used to illustrate the chords are very easy to read. The frame depicts a portion of the guitar's fretboard. The vertical lines represent the strings of the guitar with the thickest strings to the left and the thinnest strings to the right. The horizontal lines represent the frets. The nut of the guitar is represented by the thick horizontal bar at the top of the diagram. The dots that appear in the frames illustrate where you should place your fingers. An ✘ above the top line indicates that the string should be muted or not played while an O above the top line indicates that the string should be played open. Small dots represent notes that are optional.

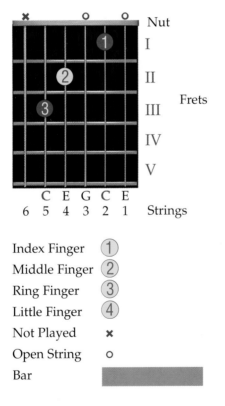

Index Finger	①
Middle Finger	②
Ring Finger	③
Little Finger	④
Not Played	✘
Open String	o
Bar	

The *Guitar Case Chord Book* groups chords in a new way that makes looking up and learning new chords easier for you. The chords are grouped by family, so the chords you're likely to find together in any one piece are next to each other in the book. You can understand how they are related at a glance.

The chord diagrams clearly indicate the position of the root and suggested fingering for each chord. There is also a special section on moveable chords.

C

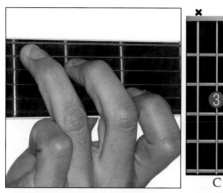
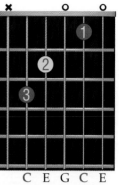

C E G C E

Cmaj7

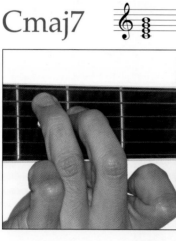
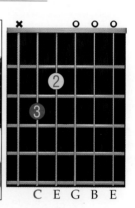

C E G B E

C6

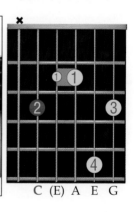

C (E) A E G

Csus4

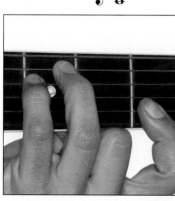
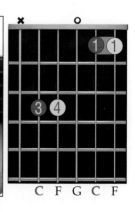

C F G C F

Dm

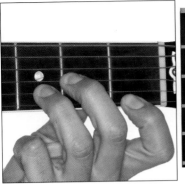
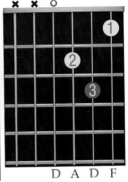

D A D F

Em

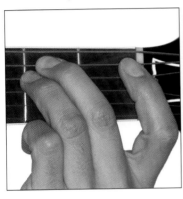
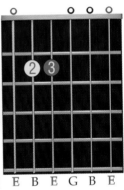

E B E G B E

F

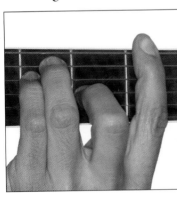
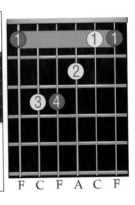

F C F A C F

G

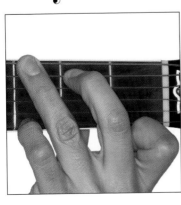
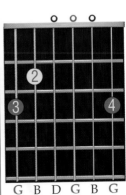

G B D G B G

Am

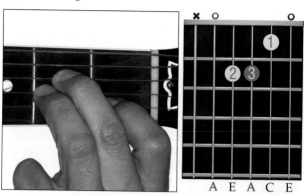

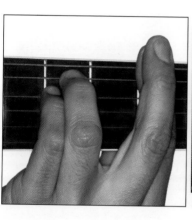

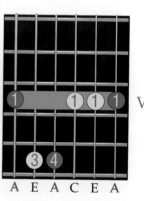

Am7

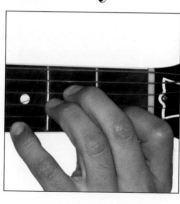

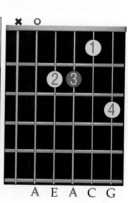

Am6

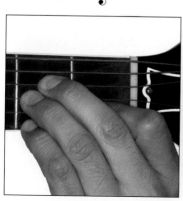

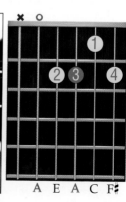

E

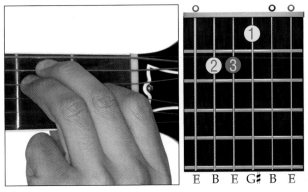

E B E G♯ B E

E7

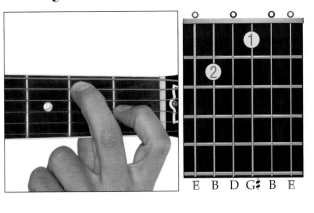

E B D G♯ B E

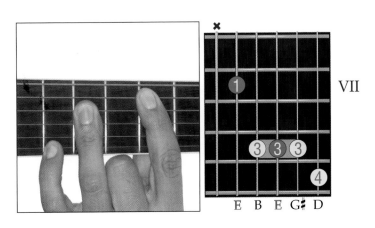

VII

E B E G♯ D

E9

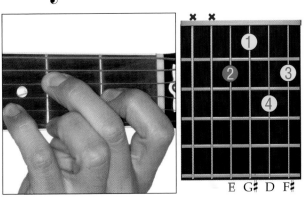

E G♯ D F♯

G

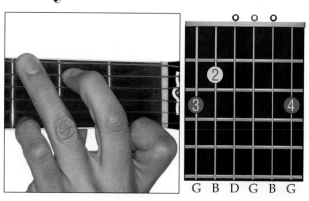

Gmaj7

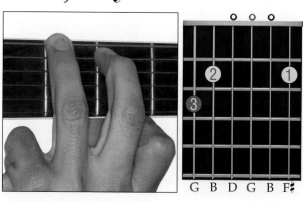

G6

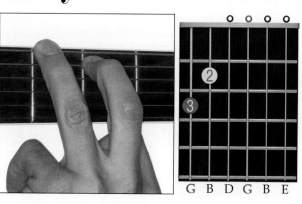

Gsus4

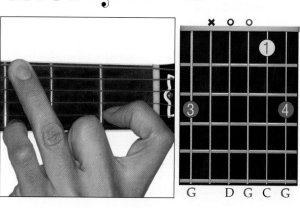

Am

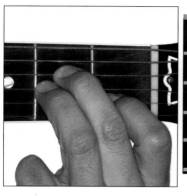

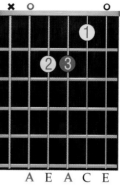

A E A C E

Bm

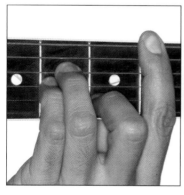

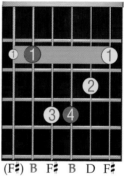

(F#) B F# B D F#

C

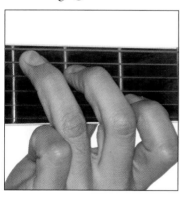

C E G C E

D

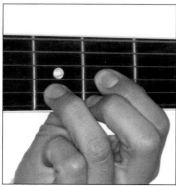

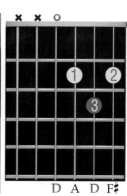

D A D F#

Em

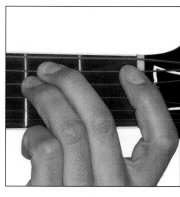

E B E G B E

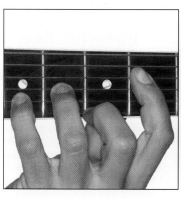
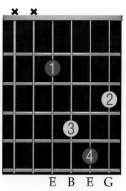

E B E G

Em7

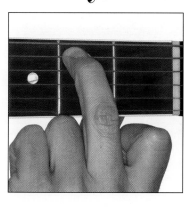

E B D G B E

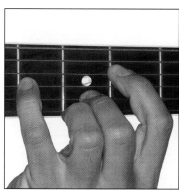
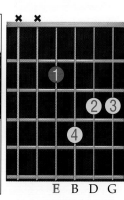

E B D G

B

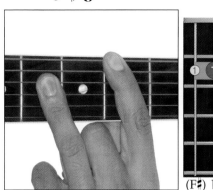
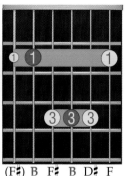

(F♯) B F♯ B D♯ F

B7

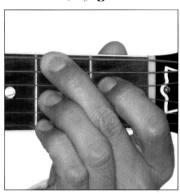

(F♯) B D♯ A B F♯

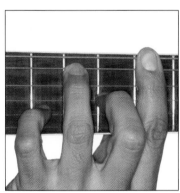
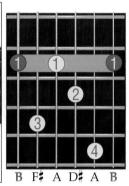

VII

B F♯ A D♯ A B

B9

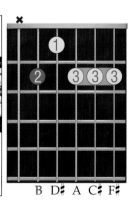

B D♯ A C♯ F♯

for songs in the key of
D

D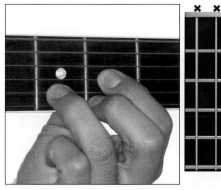

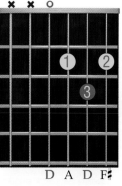

D A D F♯

Dmaj7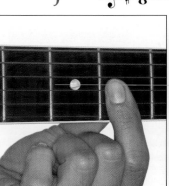

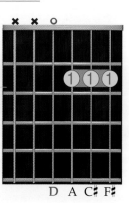

D A C♯ F♯

D6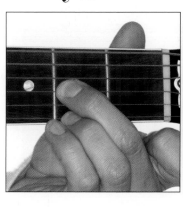

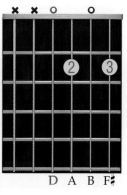

D A B F♯

Dsus4

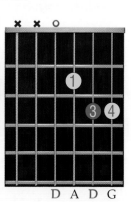

D A D G

Em

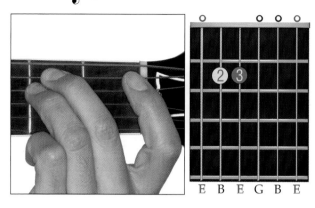

E B E G B E

F#m

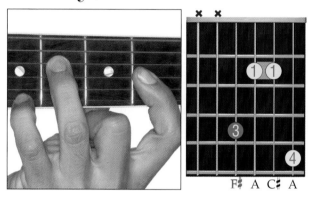

F# A C# A

G

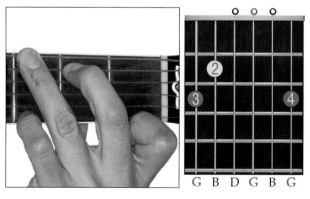

G B D G B G

A

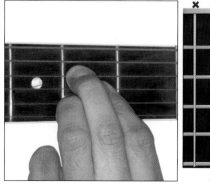
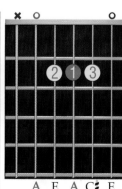

A E A C# E

Bm

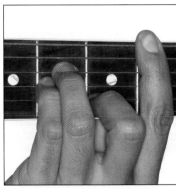
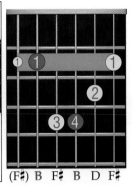

(F♯) B F♯ B D F♯

VII

B F♯ B D F♯ B

Bm7

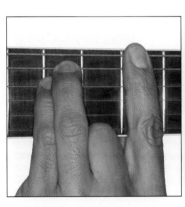
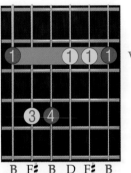

B D A B F♯

Bm6

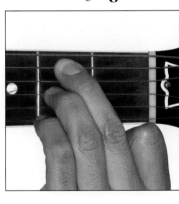
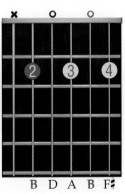

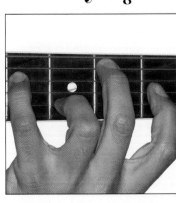
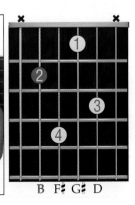

B F♯ G♯ D

F#

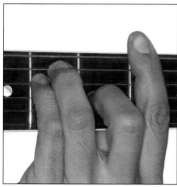

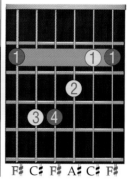

F# C# F# A# C# F#

F#7

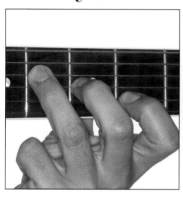

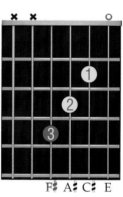

F# A# C# E

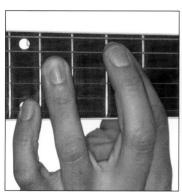

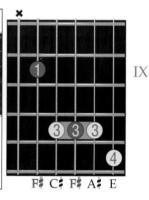

IX

F# C# F# A# E

F#9

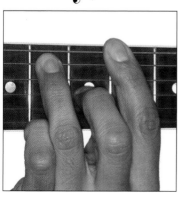

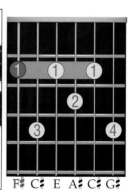

F# C# E A# C# G#

A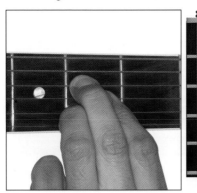

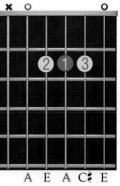

A E A C# E

Amaj7

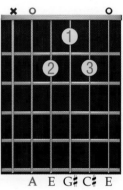

A E G# C# E

A6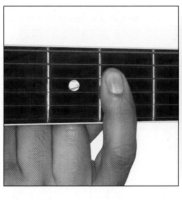

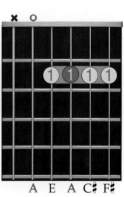

A E A C# F#

Asus4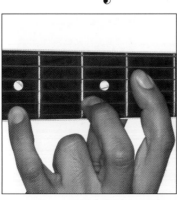

A E A D A

Bm

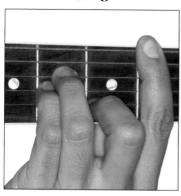

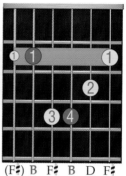

(F#) B F# B D F#

C#m

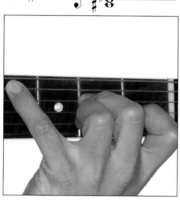

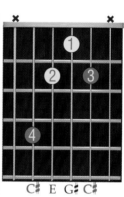

C# E G# C#

D

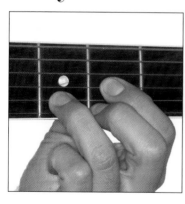

D A D F#

E

E B E G# B E

F#m
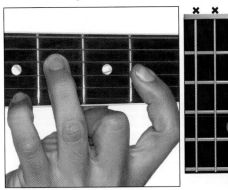
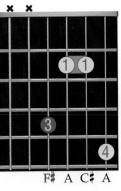

F# A C# A

F#m7

F# E A C#

C#
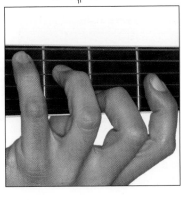
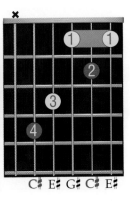

C# E# G# C# E#

C#7

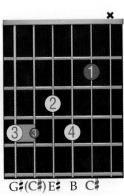

G#(C#) E# B C#

E

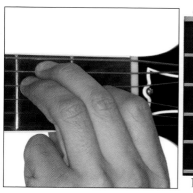
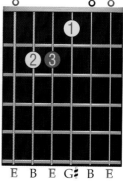

E B E G# B E

Emaj7

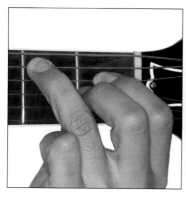
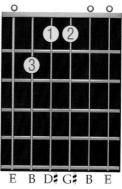

E B D# G# B E

E6

E C# E G# B E

Esus4

E B E A B E

for songs in the key of
E

F#m
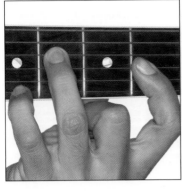
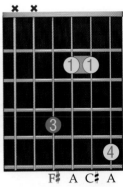

F# A C# A

G#m
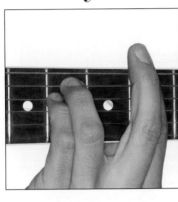
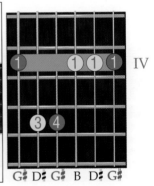

IV

G# D# G# B D# G#

A
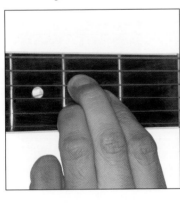

A E A C# E

B
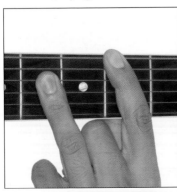
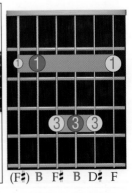

(F#) B F# B D# F

C♯m

C♯ E G♯ C♯

C♯m7

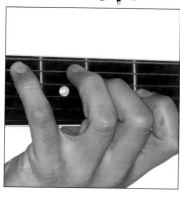

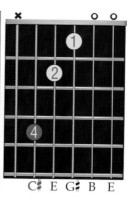

C♯ E G♯ B E

G♯

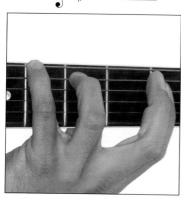

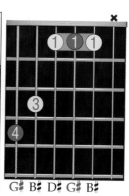

G♯ B♯ D♯ G♯ B♯

G♯7

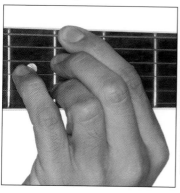

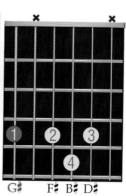

G♯ F♯ B♯ D♯

B

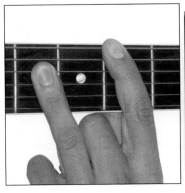
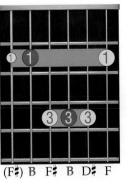

(F#) B F# B D# F

Bmaj7

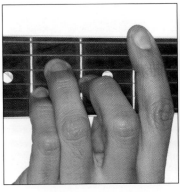
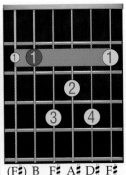

(F#) B F# A# D# F#

E

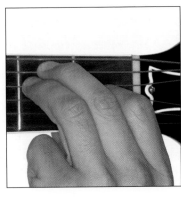

E B E G# B E

F#

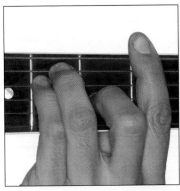

F# C# F# A# C# F#

G♯m

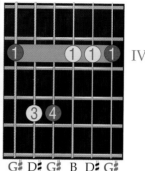

G♯ D♯ G♯ B D♯ G♯

IV

G♯m7

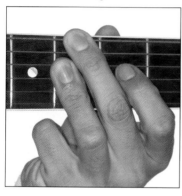
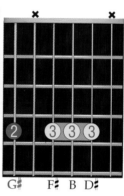

G♯   F♯ B D♯

D♯

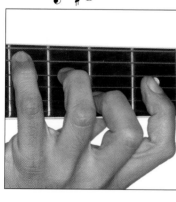
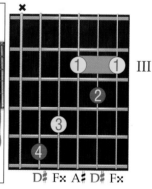

III

D♯ F× A♯ D♯ F×

D♯7

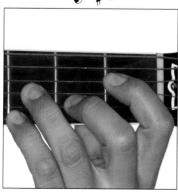
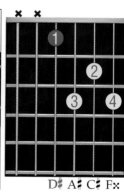

D♯ A♯ C♯ F×

G♭

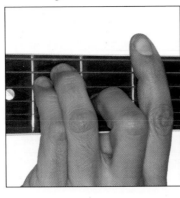
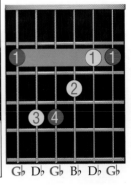

G♭ D♭ G♭ B♭ D♭ G♭

G♭maj7

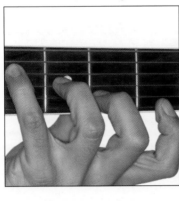
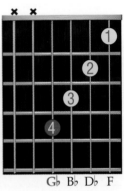

G♭ B♭ D♭ F

C♭

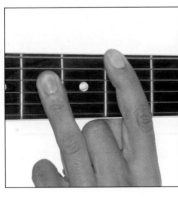
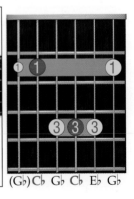

(G♭) C♭ G♭ C♭ E♭ G♭

D♭

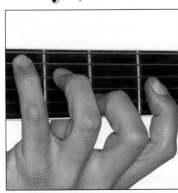
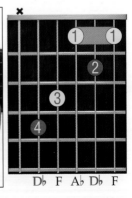

D♭ F A♭ D♭ F

E♭m

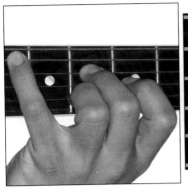
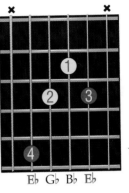

E♭ G♭ B♭ E♭

VI

E♭m6

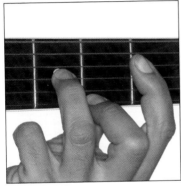
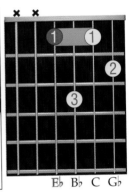

E♭ B♭ C G♭

B♭

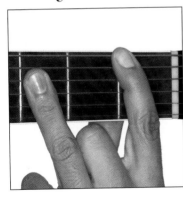
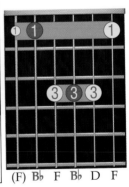

(F) B♭ F B♭ D F

B♭7

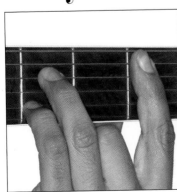
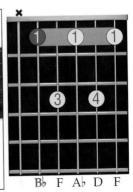

B♭ F A♭ D F

D♭

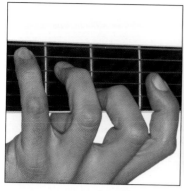
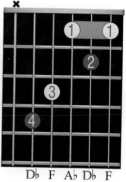

D♭ F A♭ D♭ F

D♭maj7

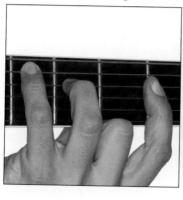

D♭ F A♭ C F

G♭

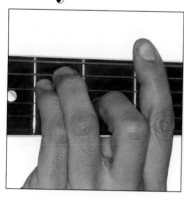
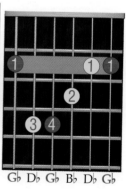

G♭ D♭ G♭ B♭ D♭ G♭

A♭7

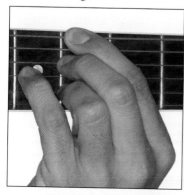
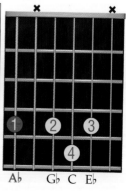

A♭ G♭ C E♭

B♭m

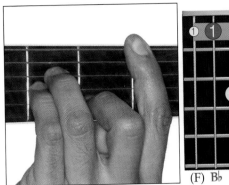

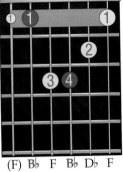

(F) B♭ F B♭ D♭ F

B♭m7

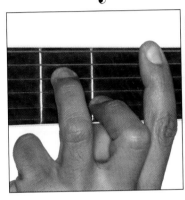

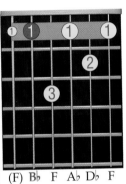

(F) B♭ F A♭ D♭ F

F

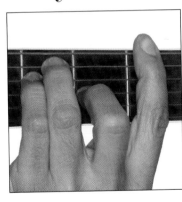

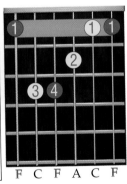

F C F A C F

F7

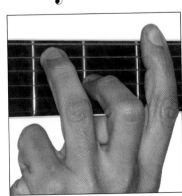

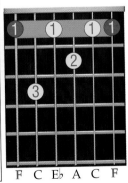

F C E♭ A C F

A♭

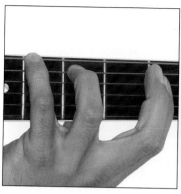

A♭ C E♭ A♭ C

A♭maj7

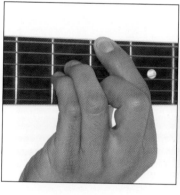
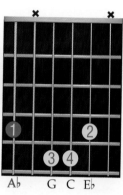

A♭ G C E♭

D♭

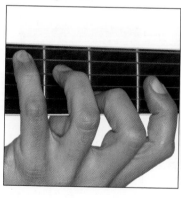
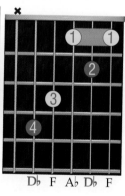

D♭ F A♭ D♭ F

E♭

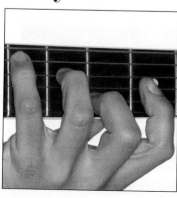
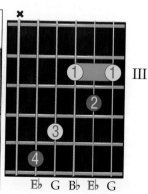

III

E♭ G B♭ E♭ G

Fm

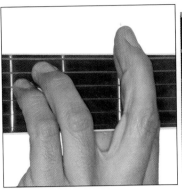

F C F A♭ C F

Fm7

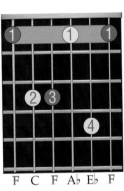

F C F A♭ E♭ F

C

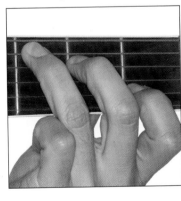

C E G C E

C7

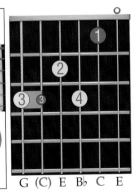

G (C) E B♭ C E

E♭

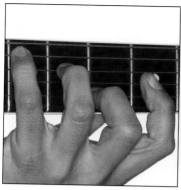

III

E♭ G B♭ E♭ G

E♭maj7

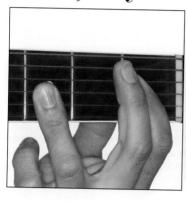

E♭ B♭ D G

A♭

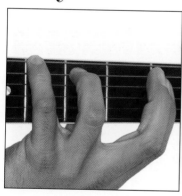

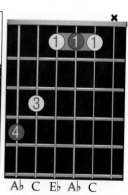

A♭ C E♭ A♭ C

B♭

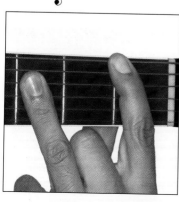

(F) B♭ F B♭ D F

Cm

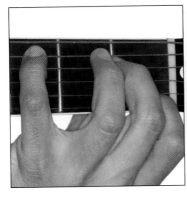
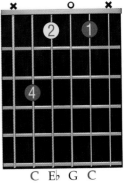

C E♭ G C

Cm7

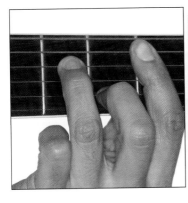
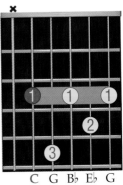

C G B♭ E♭ G

G

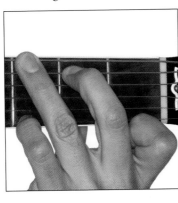
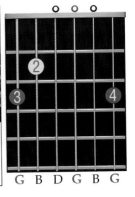

G B D G B G

G7

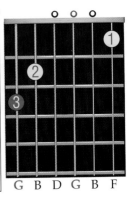

G B D G B F

B♭

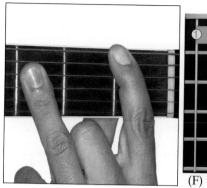

(F) B♭ F B♭ D F

B♭maj7

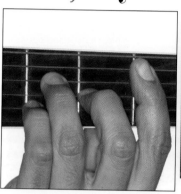
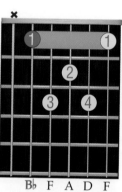

B♭ F A D F

E♭

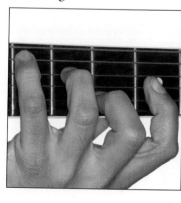

III

E♭ G B♭ E♭ G

F

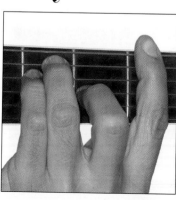
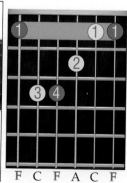

F C F A C F

Gm

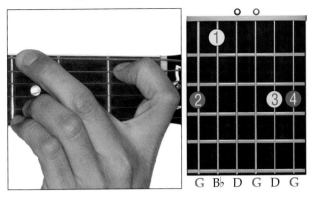

G Bb D G D G

Gm7

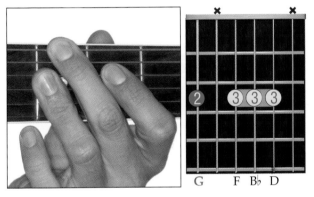

G F Bb D

D

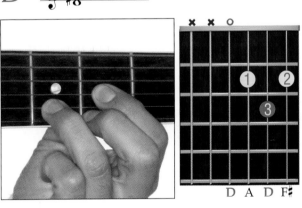

D A D F#

D7

D A C F#

F

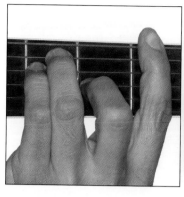

F C F A C F

Fmaj7

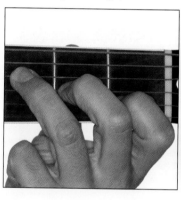

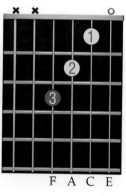

F A C E

B♭

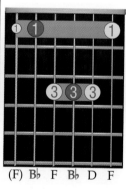

(F) B♭ F B♭ D F

C

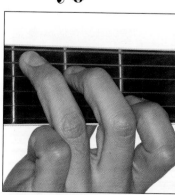

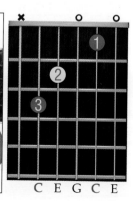

C E G C E

Dm

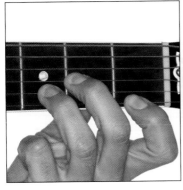

D A D F

Dm7

D A C F

A

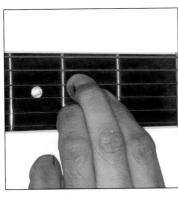
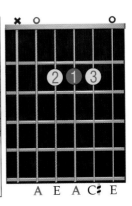

A E A C# E

A7

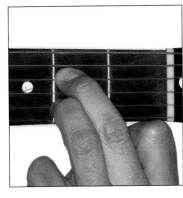
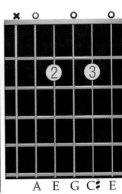

A E G C# E

major

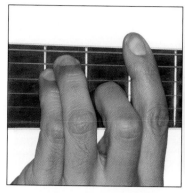 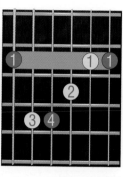

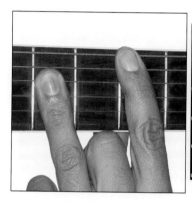 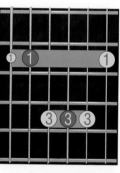

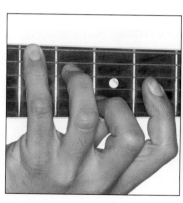 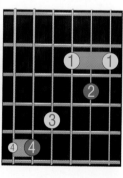

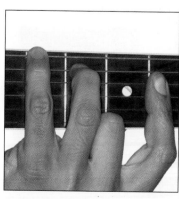 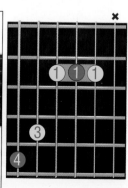

sus4

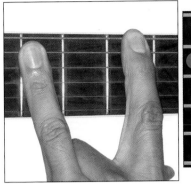 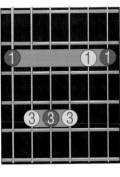

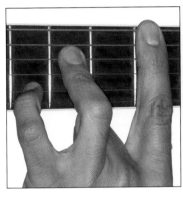 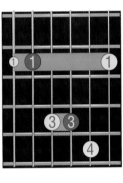

6

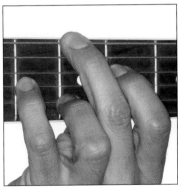 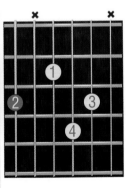

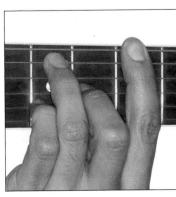 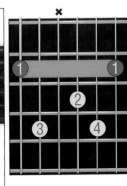

6 (cont'd)

 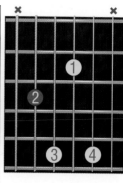

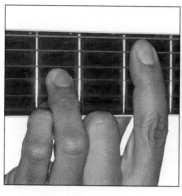 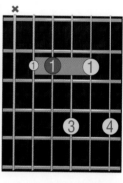

8

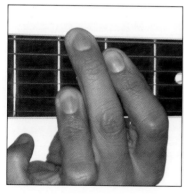 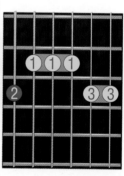

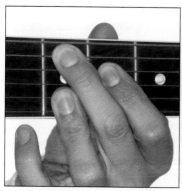 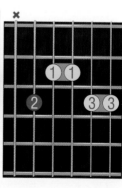

maj7

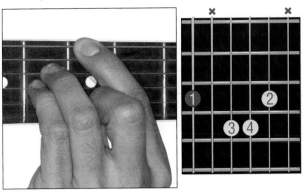

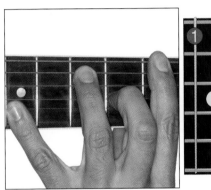
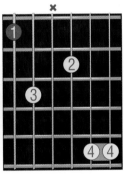

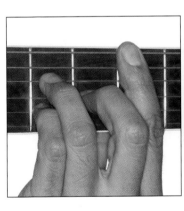
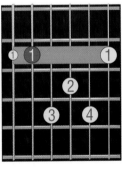

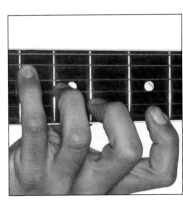
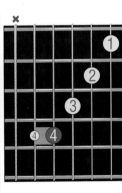

minor

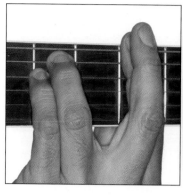 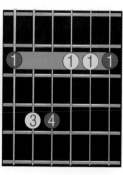

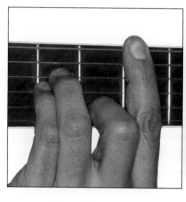 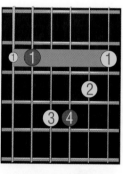

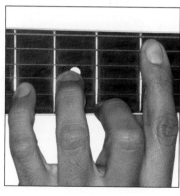 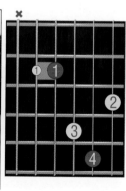

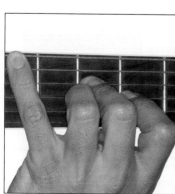 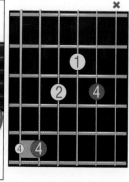

m6

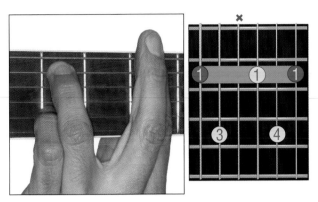

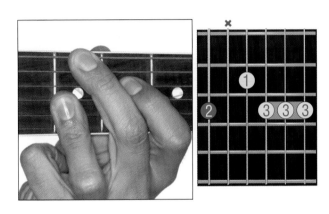

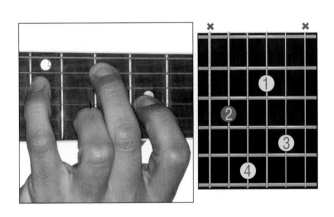

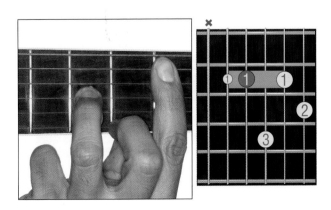

m7

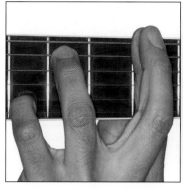 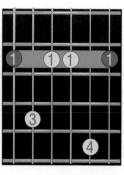

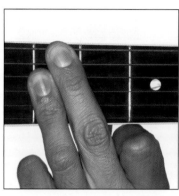 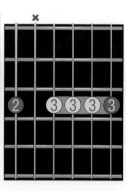

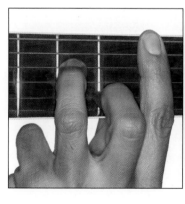 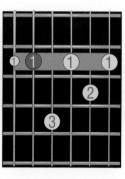

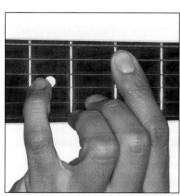 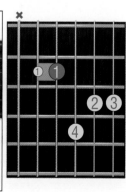

m(maj7)

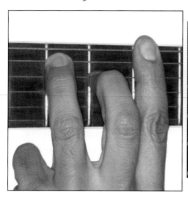 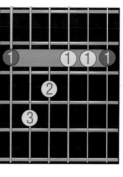

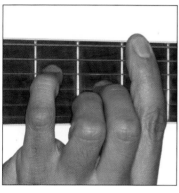 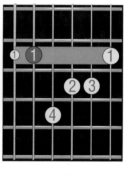

m9

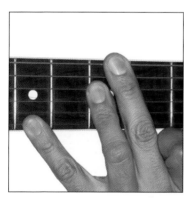 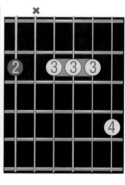

 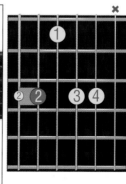

m7♭5

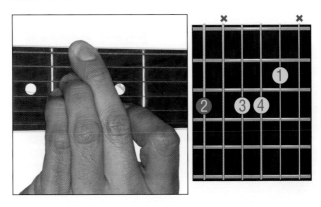

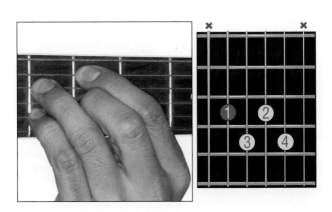

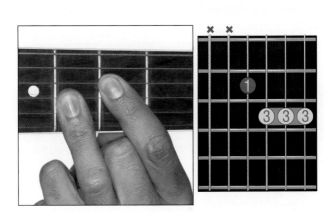

°**7** *

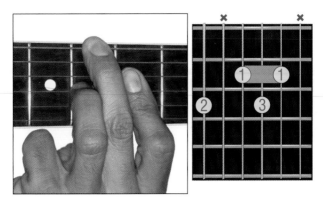

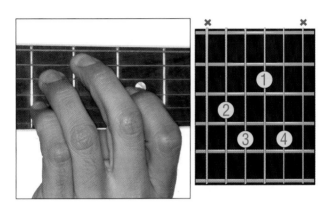

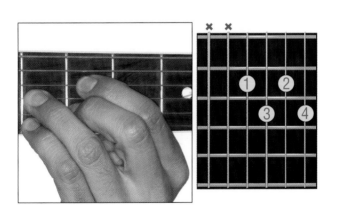

* Any note of the chord may be the root of the °7.

7

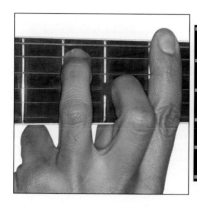 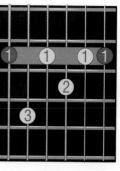

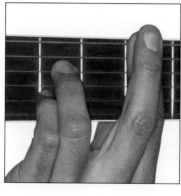 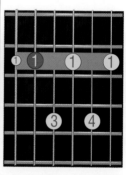

7sus4

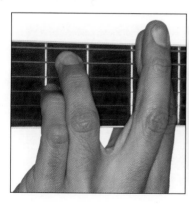 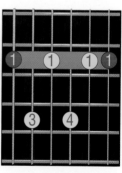

 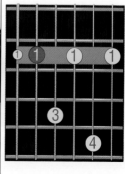

9

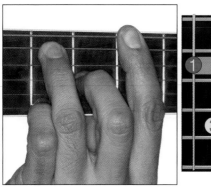 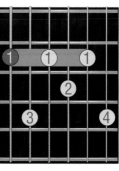

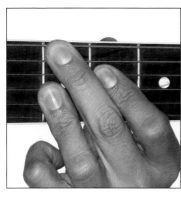 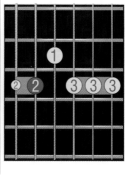

9sus4

 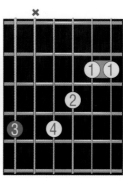

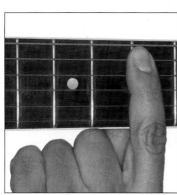 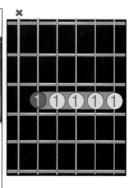

common chord symbols

Symbols used in this book	Chord Name	Alternate Symbols
Maj	Major	M; Major
m	minor	min; –
6	Major Sixth	Maj6; M6
m6	minor sixth	min6; –6
6/9	six-nine	6(add9); Maj6(add9); M6(add9)
maj7	Major seventh	M7; Maj7; Δ
7	dominant seventh	
m7	minor seventh	min7; –7
m(maj7)	minor with Major seventh	m(maj7); min(Maj7); m(+7); –(M7); min(add M7)
m7♭5	half-diminished seventh	½dim; ½dim7; ø7; m7(–5)
°7	diminished seventh	°; dim; dim7
7+	augmented seventh	+7; 7(♯5); 7(+5)
7♭5	dominant seventh with flat(ted) fifth	7(–5)
9	dominant ninth	7(add9)
maj9	Major ninth	maj9; Δ(add9); Maj7(add9);M7(add9)
7♭9	dominant flat(ted) ninth	7(add♭9); 7–9; –9
m11	minor eleventh	min11; min7(add11); m7(add11)
maj7♯11	Major seven sharp eleventh	(+11); Δ(+11); M7(+11); Δ(♯11); M7(♯11)
13	dominant thirteenth	7(add13); 7(add6)
maj13	Major thirteenth	Δ(add13); Maj7(add13); M7(add13); M7(add6)
m13	minor thirteenth	–13; min7(add13); m7(add13); –7(add13); m7(add6)
sus4	suspended fourth	(sus4)
+	augmented	aug; (♯5); +5

enharmonic equivalents

A♯ = B♭

B = C♭

B♯ = C

C♯ = D♭

D♯ = E♭

E = F♭

E♯ = F

F♯ = G♭

G♯ = A♭